Sparky
THE
Bog Dog

JANET DiLeo WADE

Illustrated by CHARLES SORRENTO

SPARKY THE BOG DOG

iUniverse books may be ordered through booksellers or by contacting:

iUniverse
1663 Liberty Drive
Bloomington, IN 47403
www.iuniverse.com
1-800-Authors (1-800-288-4677)

Because of the dynamic nature of the internet, any web addresses or links contained in this book may have changed since publication and may no longer be valid. The views expressed in this work are solely those of the author and do not necessarily reflect the views of the publisher, and the publisher hereby disclaims any responsibility for them.

Any people depicted in stock imagery provided by Getty Images are models, and such images are being used for illustrative purposes only.
Certain stock imagery © Getty Images.

ISBN: 978-1-5320-6061-8 (sc)
ISBN: 978-1-5320-6060-1 (e)

Library of Congress Control Number: 2018912267

Print information available on the last page.

iUniverse rev. date: 11/16/2018

To Sparky's playmates Ben, Field, Genevieve, Hunter and Pippa—
and all my grandchildren to come—with much love.

It was a blustery Christmas Eve when our daughter Lauren reached the cranberry bog farm. She saw the lamppost light burning brightly, guiding her way down Snapping Turtle Lane. There, our family was waiting for her to start our celebration at Mimi and Grandpa's farmhouse.

A curl of smoke was coming from the chimney, mixing with the aroma of wassail, freshly baked bread, and roast beef for dinner. Bundled up in a warm woolen hat, scarf, and coat, she quickly carried a wiggling parcel up the front porch steps.

Hearing her stomping boots, Grandpa excitedly opened the door for Lauren, and into the house charged a black-and-white ball of fur with brown eyes like saucers. Adults and children alike laughed and shouted with happy surprise as the lovable shih tzu jumped onto my lap and began licking my face and hands. Lauren had known the dog needed a loving home, and Grandpa had been able to adopt him.

But he took to me immediately, and from that moment on, he was referred to as "Mimi's dog." On the spot, I named him Sparky because he was friendly and fun and filled the room with energy.

Born in Louisiana, Sparky had been used to hot, humid weather, but in the next few weeks, he quickly made a home for himself in New England. He raced down the front walkway, sliding on the ice.

He hopped and jumped through the snow like a rabbit. The drifts were bigger than he was. Grandpa and I laughed when we heard his excited bark and saw his black coat going up and down amid the piles of snow.

Our house is next to a pretty pond surrounded by pine, oak, and maple trees. In midwinter, the pond freezes, and we cross-country ski across the snow-covered ice from one side of the pond to the other. Sparky enjoyed trotting along next to us in the cold, crisp air.

One day, a big golden retriever spotted Sparky on the ice and bounded across the pond to chase him. The retriever stopped in front of him and barked loudly. Sparky stopped, looked up at him, and barked back as if to say, "Who do you think you are? This is my pond. I'm not afraid of you."

After a few minutes, the big golden retriever ran off. Sparky followed him, and they chased each other around and around while Grandpa and I enjoyed skiing through the soft snow.

Gradually, the sun shined longer, and the days became warmer. Sparky spent many hours exploring the woods around our farmhouse. The trees here are home to red cardinals, blue jays, red-breasted robins, and small brown sparrows.

Flocks of geese flew over the pond, returning to their nesting grounds. Families of ducks swam in the pond and bobbed for fish and insects to eat.

One warm spring day, I went kayaking on the pond. I spent the morning paddling through the calm water, lily pads, and vines. Toward noon, I decided to return to the shore to have lunch.

Suddenly, I heard a big splash. I looked ahead to see a huge frog in the lily pads. But coming closer, I saw it wasn't a frog. It was Sparky! His black head, with his big brown eyes and little pink tongue, was bobbing among the lily pads as he gasped for air, treading water, trying to reach me!

I glided over to him, scooped him up into the kayak, and paddled to shore. We were both muddy and covered with vines, but Sparky was happy to be saved.

Sparky came to consider the woods and pond as his own. Several times each day, he paraded over the lawn, head held high, looking for visitors, friends, and new adventures.

He trotted after delivery trucks and waited for a dog biscuit from the mailman.

Throughout the year, snapping turtles slowly plod along the lane, looking for a place to lay their eggs. At first, Sparky didn't know what to make of them. When he went up to sniff one, it pulled in its head and feet. It resembled a gray rock!

Over time, Sparky became comfortable sniffing his way through the woods, often seeing a deer nibbling at leaves or a family of wild turkeys scratching for food. They all got along well and didn't bother each other.

But rabbits were different! Sparky barked and chased after them. Many times, they tried to eat plants in Grandpa's garden.

One day, Grandpa was trying to catch a rabbit using a cage with a carrot and lettuce, but Grandpa was outsmarted by the rabbit, who was able to get the food and not get trapped! Sparky finally chased the rabbit away, saving Grandpa's garden from being destroyed.

On a pretty summer day, I was weeding in the garden. Sparky was doing his daily walk around the property when he spotted a frog. The bumpy brown frog sat still and looked up at Sparky.

Sparky stood still and bent down to sniff him. The frog jumped forward, and Sparky jumped back. It was so funny that I laughed and laughed.

One of Sparky's favorite things to do was to roll in the grass and dirt at the end of Snapping Turtle Lane. I would get very frustrated because I had to give him a lot of baths so he'd be clean enough to come into the house.

Sparky hated baths. He liked mud but not soap and clean water. After I would soap up his black-and-white fur, he wiggled and shook and got me all wet.

He liked that I used my hair drier to fluff up his coat. It felt nice and warm. In the hot weather, he would lie on the front porch and dry off in the sun. He liked that even better!

I called Sparky my "doorbell." He barked whenever someone drove down the lane and came to the door. He made me feel safe—my own personal guard dog.

When our grandchildren came to visit, he would trot along with them as they rode their bicycles in the quiet lane and would excitedly run around in circles on the lawn as they played chase. After a long day of "keeping watch," he would snore soundly, outstretched on the floor next to their beds.

Autumn on the bogs is beautiful. Orange and gold leaves cover the maples and oaks. When the cranberries are ready to be harvested, the bogs are flooded with water from the pond.

The red berries float to the top, where they are collected, and then they are taken to market to be sold. Sparky enjoyed walking along the ridge of the bogs sniffing the cranberries.

One afternoon, Sparky went out for his routine walk, but he did not come home. After an hour of waiting for him to return to the house, I got worried. Putting on my jacket and boots, I walked around the edge of all the bogs.

I called out, "Sparky, come!" but there was no response. It got colder, and the sun soon would set. I was afraid to think of Sparky scared and shivering out in the bogs alone.

I went back to the house and put on a hat and gloves. I wasn't going to give up searching for Sparky. The sun set over the pond, the sky faded pink and orange. I was walking on the edge of the front bog near the house when I heard a faint bark.

I looked down among the vines leading to the floating cranberries. There, I saw Sparky, wet and shaking.

Climbing down into the bog, I picked up my cold, muddy, scared little dog. He squirmed in my arms and licked my hands and face.

I quickly carried him up the bank and down the lane to the farmhouse, where I wrapped him in a warm, soft blanket. We sat in my favorite chair by the fireplace. The normally frisky dog snuggled in my lap for a long time.

Sparky the bog dog was safely home.